Pray in This Way

BOOKS IN THE PROTESTANT PULPIT EXCHANGE®

Pray in This Way

Sermons on the Lord's Prayer

John A. Stroman

PROTESTANT
PULPIT
EXCHANGE

Abingdon Press
Nashville

PRAY IN THIS WAY: SERMONS ON THE LORD'S PRAYER

Copyright © 1995 by Abingdon Press

This book is printed on recycled, acid-free paper.

Library of Congress Cataloging-in-Publication Data

Stroman, John A.
    Pray in this way : sermons on the Lord's prayer / John A. Stroman.
       p.   cm.—(Protestant pulpit exchange)
    Includes bibliographical references.
    ISBN 0-687-00234-6 (alk. paper)
    1. Lord's prayer—Sermons. 2. Sermons, American. I. Title.
  II. Series.
  BV230.S783   1994
  226.9'606—dc20   94-38858
                                           CIP

Scripture quotations noted NRSV are from the New Revised Standard Version Bible, Copyright 1989 by the Division of Christian Education of the National Council of the Churches of Christ in the USA. Used by permission.

The poem on p. 25 is from *Also My Journey*, by Marguerite H. Atkins. Copyright © 1985 by Marguerite H. Atkins. Used by permission of Morehouse Publishing.

94 95 96 97 98 99 00 01 02 03—10 9 8 7 6 5 4 3 2 1

MANUFACTURED IN THE UNITED STATES OF AMERICA

In appreciation
for
Samuel Kofi Osabutey
and the members of
Ebenezer Methodist Church
Ada Foah, Ghana, West Africa

You taught me the meaning of
Christian discipleship

Contents

Preface

hy yet another book on the Lord's Prayer? Because that is the nature of Scripture. It is always given to interpretation. Also the task of the preacher is to bring new, fresh insight to the old, old story.

There has been an undiminished stream of commentaries and paraphrases of the Lord's Prayer from every period of the church's history. Each age must seek to discover the meaning of the gospel for itself. Every age must look again at this classic prayer, which Thomas Aquinas noted in his day was the perfect prayer, since it came from the lips of Jesus in response to his disciples' request, "Lord, teach us to pray."

My purpose is to engage the reader in serious thought and meditation regarding the Lord's Prayer and to prompt the question, What do these words mean? or more important, What do they mean to me?

I want to thank the people who have made this work possible. A special thanks to Leona Irvine and to my wife, Vivian, who painstakingly helped prepare this manuscript for publication. Also, to the members of Pasadena Community Church, who give to me such thoughtful and prayerful support in my weekly task of sermon preparation. These chapters were my attempt to rethink the Lord's Prayer with the Pasadena congregation during the Lenten season. Their insights and comments have been invaluable and encouraging.

At the end of the book, I have listed resources that may be helpful to those who would like to engage in further study.

John A. Stroman
Pasadena Community Church
St. Petersburg, Florida

Introduction

*T*he Lord's Prayer stands at the very heart and center of Jesus' teaching. There is no other prayer of such sheer power and majesty. It is the most effective summary of the Christian faith, covering every aspect of New Testament theology, dealing with the kingdom of God, forgiveness, temptation, daily living, and deliverance. It is concerned with the whole world from our daily bread to the coming of the kingdom. The Lord's Prayer is for everyone.

There is hardly a moment when it is not being repeated somewhere on the earth, from the hospital room to the graveside, from the baptismal font to the marriage ceremony, from the worship service to private devotions. From the great cathedrals to remote shanties, it is being spoken in nearly every language known to men and women across the world. It is spoken by children and adults, the poor and the powerful, the religious and not so religious, the simple and the wise.

Brevity and Simplicity

The Lord's Prayer is unique because of its brevity and simplicity. In Matthew's account it numbers barely fifty words, and in Luke's account merely thirty-five words. The Pharisees were accustomed to praying long, complicated prayers. They felt they would find audience with God because of their "much speaking." By using the Lord's Prayer, Jesus sought, in the words of Steve Harper (*Praying Through the Lord's Prayer* [Nashville: Upper Room, 1992]) to "uncomplicate prayer" and to free it from the notion that longer is better. Through design, Jesus focused on a model for prayer that is short, understandable, and contains everyday words that are readily comprehended by the masses. Jesus wants our hearts, rather than our understanding, to be the foundation of our prayers.

The disciples requested this prayer. There was confusion about what prayer was in their minds and within the Jewish community in Jesus' time. Jesus was dealing with this confusion about prayer itself when he gave his disciples this pattern for prayer. His response to their request was a prayer so simple that it could be memorized by children, yet at the same time, so profound that scholars have spent lifetimes exploring its message and have written volumes in an attempt to express its meaning and implications.

The thing we must not overlook in our study of the Lord's Prayer is that Jesus gave it to us so that we could pray more effectively. Steve Harper is right on target when he suggests that the Lord's Prayer releases us from some hurdles and obstacles that can keep us from praying. It reveals to us the motivation for real prayer. It is an invitation to prayer.

In the Lord's Prayer, Jesus is simply making it easier for us to pray. Paradoxically, we yearn for prayer, yet we avoid it. We are attracted to it, yet we ignore it. Prayer is something we want to do and feel we should do. It is as if there is a great chasm between our desire to pray and our actually engaging in meaningful prayer. But prayer requires no special language, location, or ability. Prayer is for everyone.

A Source of Unity

The Lord's Prayer rises as a great choral symphony from all of the people on earth before the throne of God. No group of words are as well known by Christians as these words, expressing so succinctly the centrality of the Christian faith and providing us a sense of unity amid the diversity of our varied languages and liturgies. In our use of the Lord's Prayer, we speak a common tongue as we join with millions around the world.

Not only does it provide unity for the diverse ecumenical church, but the Lord's Prayer also provides a sense of cohesiveness for our lives. It makes an impact on every moment of life, from birth to baptism to confirmation to marriage and death. At these pressure points in our lives, we repeat the Lord's Prayer.

The Lord's Prayer deals with the necessities of our lives and in doing so expresses a remarkable unity for life. It deals with the three essential needs that all of us have: for bread, for forgiveness, and for deliverance from temptation. In the expression of these needs, the prayer is carefully crafted so that it lays all of life—past, present, and future—before God. Bread is our most pressing *present* need, and it includes all that is essential for the maintenance of life. Forgiveness is a release from the *past* that keeps us in bondage. The deliverance from evil is committing the *future* into the hands of God. When we come to that moment of potential failure we pray, "O Lord, be with us, deliver us through these treacherous mine fields that we must travel."

Special Problems for the Preacher

Preaching a series of sermons on the Lord's Prayer poses special problems. First, we need to ask ourselves, How can I preach on a subject that is so familiar? What can I possibly say that has not already been said? How can I face something so familiar with new insight and freshness? It took me by surprise during a recent Lenten series on the Lord's Prayer that the people eagerly received these sermons. The congregation expressed interest and anticipation for each week's sermon, and their enthusiasm inspired me throughout the entire series. What they seemed to be saying to me was, "I have been repeating these words all of my life, and I am not sure what I have been saying." One person told me that even though the Lord's Prayer has been around for centuries, he was convinced that it has something important to say to him, and he was anxious to discover what it was. But for many people familiarity often puts a glaze over their eyes.

Second, there is a mood among us that worship, liturgy, and music ought to be relevant and up to date. The phrase "contemporary worship" has become a catchword. We are eagerly trying to update our expressions of faith, our forms of worship, hymns, and prayers. Such renewal is desirable, especially as the church seeks to reach the unchurched, the baby boomers, and the secular. But in our desire for a "contemporary worship experience" we may be tempted to replace the Lord's Prayer with a prayer that is vernacular and up to date. At the same time, we may be underestimating a vital religious factor in every generation—the power of the familiar and the power of tradition to inspire hope for the future.

Should we eliminate everything in our worship that is not immediately understood to anyone who enters? Leander E. Keck expresses caution at this point in his book *The Church Confident,* stating that much of the liturgical change has amounted to little more than "a substitution of the trivial for the ossified." He goes on to conclude that far too often, our churches are indeed "caught in the act," engaged in worship that is "thoroughly secularized" (Keck, *The Church Confident* [Nashville: Abingdon Press, 1993], 25).

Familiarity as an Asset

One of the absolutely essential elements in meaningful worship is the grip of the familiar. It not only conveys overtones of religious meaning that reach us in no other way but also provides for us the rest for the mind and spirit without which true worship is impossible. Wade Clark Roof, in his book *A Generation of Seekers* (San Francisco: Harper, 1993), a study of the spiritual journey of baby boomers, points out that for a sizable number of boomers, life goes on pretty much as it always has. They are very much embedded in traditional religious life. For them, congregations provide a "community of memory." Roof concludes, "Traditions pull at all of us, and for many boomers these are powerful forces, in no way to be minimized. Congregations are familiar places where they find meaning and belonging and a spiritual home" (p. 251).

David H. C. Read said that he had never been asked to perform a "contemporary" funeral service. Neither have I. But on numerous occasions I have been asked to use Psalm 23, John 14, or Romans 8 and to be sure to include the Lord's Prayer, to be either sung or said. Read points out that it is quite remarkable that Jesus Christ, the great innovator, the disturber of the status quo, made sure that his disciples through the years ahead would have something enduring and familiar. He taught them the Lord's Prayer. Just prior to his teaching it, he warned against "empty phrases" and "vain repetitions," but he knew the value of familiar words. He most likely repeated three times a day the familiar *Shema:*

INTRODUCTION

"Hear, O Israel, the Lord thy God is one God." Even in these days of enormously great change we still respond to the tug of the familiar.

Although the familiarity of the Lord's Prayer may cause it to become trite and repetitious, the preacher is faced with the opportunity of bridging the gap between the familiarity of the prayer and the new meaning it can have for our world and our day. The preacher is challenged to bring new wine for the old wineskins, new insight and freshness to old, familiar words and phrases.

Although we have the problem of familiarity, it is healthy for us to periodically focus our attention on these words and discover their significance for today. This book is the result of my attempt to do this through a series of sermons I preached at Pasadena Community Church, St. Petersburg, Florida, during Lent. I share these words and thoughts, trusting that they will be a source of greater discovery and insight for others.

Pray in This Way

CHAPTER ONE

> *"Pray then in this way: Our Father in heaven . . ."*
> *(Matt. 6:9)*

God–Intimate and Close

Jesus' sense of God was so close, so real, and so intimate that he never prayed without addressing God as his heavenly Father. His relationship with God was always expressed from a father-son relationship. This familiar and ideal relationship has nurtured Christian prayer for centuries. But addressing God as "Father" creates a great deal of uneasiness in today's world.

Paul Tillich, in his book *The Dynamics of Faith* (New York: Harper, 1957), states that all of our language about God is symbolic, "because symbolic language alone is able to express the ultimate" (p. 41). In our attempt to describe God we use metaphors, similes, parables, and poetry. In describing God's comfort, I think of the words of Isaiah 32:2, where the prophet talks about "the shade of a great rock in a weary land." In describing God's power, I think of Martin Luther's hymn "A Mighty Fortress Is Our God." In talking about the guidance and care of God, immediately the Twenty-third Psalm comes to mind, "The LORD is my shepherd." To describe God's personal relationship with us and the world, the most popular metaphor through the ages has been that of "father" and the "fatherhood of God." For centuries we have prayed, "Our father, who art in heaven . . ." and confessed our faith together by saying, "I believe in God the Father Almighty . . ." These metaphors—shadow, rock, fortress, shepherd, and father—have served us well in our attempt to understand and to describe God.

In his book, *The Idea of the Holy* (New York: Oxford University Press, 1928), Rudolph Otto reminds us that it is impossible for the finite human mind to comprehend the infinite eternal God. He states, "If the human mind could fully explain God, then God would cease to exist" (p. 71). For to be God, God has to be illusive, mysterious, and distant. The Lord declared to Isaiah:

> For as the heavens are higher than the earth,
> so are my ways higher than your ways
> and my thoughts than your thoughts.
> (Isa. 55:9)

Our desire to communicate to others the reality of God makes the use of symbols and metaphors necessary. In our cautious and inadequate expressions, we must keep in mind that God will remain far more than our words and phrases.

This can be a risky business. A little girl in Sunday school was working very hard on a drawing. The teacher asked her what she was doing. The girl said she was drawing a picture of God. The teacher told her that no one knows what God looks like. Confidently the girl replied, "They will when I am done." When we speak, we may feel that not only do we have a picture of God, but also that our picture is the only picture of God. Upon realizing that our language of God is symbolic, we may feel that our preferred symbol or metaphor is the only one. We are so limited in our expression because our finite minds are trying to express the infinite. We may distort the image of God by the limitations of the symbols we use.

Upon realizing that our language of God is symbolic, we may feel that our preferred symbol or metaphor is the only one.

Jesus calls God "Father," and it is impossible for us to use a symbol that would convey the same idea of this divine relationship to all people everywhere. For centuries, Christians have thought of God as the "eternal masculine." So we ask the obvious question, Why have Christians overlooked the "mother" metaphor for God?

There is an obvious answer to that. The Bible reflects the period in which it was written. The biblical metaphors for God as "Father," "King," and "Lord" were used in a time when the male-dominated monarchy was the keystone of political order. God's sovereignty was expressed in terms of royalty and kingship.

In the agricultural society of the first century, it was inevitable that the poetic imagery of God's tender care and concern should be drawn from a shepherd and his flock. This imagery was well known to the people of Jesus' day, who encountered shepherds and sheep every day. To them, this imaging of God was vivid. Sheep and shepherds are not so well known to our world.

In the patriarchal society of Jesus' day, the father figure was dominant, especially first-century Jewish families. It is quite natural that their thoughts of God would center around God as heavenly Father. These verbal images and metaphors functioned well for those days. But the world has changed. To say that God is our Father conveys entirely different meanings in today's world. Because of the abusiveness of some fathers, for many children today, the father image is terrifying and frightening.

A chaplain at a children's home told how he could not use the Lord's Prayer at the home. There was a thirteen-year-old girl at the home who, from the age of seven, had been repeatedly abused by her father. Whenever she heard the word *father*, it triggered a violent reaction from her. Thus to use *father* as a metaphor for God is not always suitable for all of the world's children.

However, we must seek to understand what this metaphor meant for Jesus and how he understood God as his heavenly Father. What did it mean for him? What does it mean for us? Jesus admonished his disciples, "Pray then in this way: Our Father in heaven."

Notice the opening word of the prayer: "Our"—not "my" or "your," but "our." For Jesus, God is the Father of all people, from the four corners of the earth. God is the common longing of the human heart. The "our" of this prayer cuts across every land, culture, race, and need. God is not the possession of any one group of people, but of all people.

Then notice that the prayer begins with God. The very first phrase of the prayer recognizes who God is. It is only when God is given proper place that all things fall into place. The very first thought of this prayer is to focus thought and recognition upon God rather than upon self, needs, or problems. If our first thoughts are on ourselves, we will be disappointed with the results of our prayer and feel that we have failed. Jesus teaches us in his prayer to get our thoughts off of ourselves and onto God, who for Jesus is "our" Father of all.

Just prior to Jesus' teaching the Lord's Prayer to his disciples he gives two general rules regarding prayer. First, Jesus criticizes those who pray to be seen and heard by others. "But whenever you pray, go into your room and shut the door and pray to your Father who is in secret" (Matt. 6:6). The story is told of the time when Harry Emerson Fosdick was invited to Boston on a Sunday evening to preach. Just prior to his sermon, a prominent

Boston pastor led in the evening prayer. Following the sermon, someone asked Fosdick what he thought of that minister's prayer. "It was the most eloquent prayer ever offered to a Boston audience," he replied.

Second, Jesus insisted that we must remember that the God to whom we pray knows what we need: "For your Father knows what you need before you ask him" (Matt. 6:8). We do not come to a God who needs to be coaxed, pestered, or battered for answers. God is a God of love, who is more ready to answer prayer than we are to pray.

Richard Foster, in his book *Prayer* (San Francisco: Harper, 1992), says that the one thing that should strike us when we read this prayer is the deep, personal, and intimate nearness of the Father God that Jesus experienced and taught. The idea of God as Father was not new to those who heard Jesus pray. In Psalm 103:13 the psalmist states:

> As a father has compassion for his children,
>   so the LORD has compassion for those
>   who fear him.

In regard to this passage, Walter Brueggemann, in his book *Biblical Perspectives on Evangelism* (Nashville: Abingdon Press, 1993) points out how striking it is that when the psalmist speaks about God's gentleness toward God's people, the image is that of a father. God is like a father in two ways. First, the father here is "motherlike," in being willing to care in inordinant ways and to stand in utter solidarity. Second, God is like a father who remembers where we came from, how we are born, of what we are made, and how utterly fragile and precarious we are.

Also, Hosea 11:1-4 talks about God as a Father who takes the children into his arms and leads them with "cords of human kindness" and the "bands of love" and "bent down to them and fed them."

The Bible does not give only Father pictures of God. Through the prophet Isaiah, God uses the language of a mother: "As a mother comforts her child,/ so I will comfort you" (66:13). It is not the image of God as a father that startles us as we read the Lord's Prayer. Rather, we are startled by the invitation to address God in such a personal and intimate manner. To the faithful Jew, who even hesitated to speak the divine name, the childlike intimacy of Jesus' words must have been utterly shocking.

The very first words that a Jewish child learns to speak are *abba* (which means "father") and *imma* (which means "mother"). The word *abba* is so personal and so familiar a term that no one ever used it to address God—until Jesus did. It has been pointed out that there is not a single example of the use of *abba* as an address to God in the whole of Jewish literature. Jesus' utter intimacy with Father God is startling. Just think about it: The God of creation; the God of Abraham, Isaac, and Jacob; the God of Sarah, Leah, and Rachel; the God of creation; the God of heaven and earth—is our Father!

In the Lord's Prayer we are invited into the same intimacy with God the Father that Jesus knew upon earth when he encouraged us to pray, "Our Father." We are encouraged to crawl into God's lap and receive God's love, comfort, healing, and strength. We can laugh and weep freely and openly in the arms of *Abba*, our Father God. We can be hugged by a caring and comforting *Imma*, our Mother God.

> *We are encouraged to crawl into God's lap and receive God's love, comfort, healing, and strength.*

The whole of Jesus' life was a prolonged *abba* experience. The real test of "our Father" thinking came on the cross. If

Jesus was wrong about his life, it would have been seen here. No crueler instrument of death ever existed. As a deterrent to crime, the Romans lined the Appian Way with crosses, on which insurrectionists and freedom fighters were crucified, reminding everyone of the price of rebellion. Jesus saw the cross and death looming before him. In Gethsemane he prayed, "O Father, if it be possible!" It wasn't possible. The masses cried out for his crucifixion. How close, real, and intimate was God the Father then? As the final hour of life approached, would Jesus abandon the idea of God as Father? No! From the cross Jesus prayed, "Father, forgive them," interceding for those who placed him there. Luke tells us that Jesus' very last words were: "Father, *Abba,* into your hands I commend my spirit." Home at last with the Father.

Marguerite Henry Atkins wrote a remarkable book entitled *Also My Journey* (Wilton, Conn.: Morehouse-Barlow, 1985), telling about her years of caring for her husband, who had Alzheimer's disease. It is a vivid account of her struggle, pain, anguish, and the hope of faith. She wrote a poem just before her husband's death.

> He is my loved one
> But Thou Lord didst create him
> and so Thou lovest him more.
> I know Thou wilt be near him
> in his death. . . .
> Thou wilt hold him close in Thy arms
> as a mother cradles her child
> while sleeping.

That loving, parental image of God brought her hope, comfort, and peace. She could visualize how in death God was near to her husband, holding him close as a mother would cradle her child.

Is not this how God cares for us? So much so, that we can experience the power and strength of *Abba*, God our Father, and the caring and comfort of *Imma*, God our Mother.

CHAPTER TWO

> *" . . . hallowed be your name." (Matt. 6:9)*

God, Who Is Holy

*W*e do not have a sense of the holy today. A man who was desperately trying to straighten the tombstone on his wife's grave was interviewed by a television reporter. The night The night before, a motorcycle gang had played havoc in the cemetery, knocking over many tombstones and desecrating gravesites. The man, in a distraught and tearful voice, asked the reporter, "Isn't anything sacred anymore?" Most people have lost touch with the concept of the sacred, the holy. We do not give much thought to the "holiness" of God's name, because we do not know about the holiness of God. In the face of such devaluation of the holiness of God, we do not seem to know what is holy or sacred anymore. Nothing appears sacred, not even the name of God.

Jesus began his prayer, "Our Father in heaven, hallowed be your name." *Hallowed* is not a common word; it has little use today. The numerous translations of the New Testament have not improved upon it. Two of the latest translations, the NIV and NRSV, still use the translation *hallowed.* Webster defines *hallowed* as "holy, sacred, or revered."

What did Jesus mean when he prayed, "hallowed be your name"? The word *hallowed* is derived from the Greek word *hagios,* which basically means "different" or "separate." A thing that is holy, *hagios,* is different from other things. A holy people are set apart from other people. A holy temple is different and set apart from other buildings. God's day is a holy day, set apart and different from other days. Add to this the fact that in Hebrew the *name* does not simply mean the name by which a person is called. In Hebrew one's name connotes the nature, character, and personality of the person so far as it is revealed or known. This is why the psalmist could say, "And those who know your name put their trust in you" (Ps. 9:10). Those who know what God is like, who know God's nature and character will trust God. "Some take pride in chariots, and some in horses, / but our pride is in the name of the LORD our God" (Ps. 20:7). Therefore, if we put both of these thoughts together, we can say: "Help us, O Lord, to give to you that special, revered place that your loving character deserves and demands."

Our knowledge of God is essential. No one will revere an immoral, uncaring, disinterested god.

The Lord's Prayer begins with this phrase because our reverence for God is based on the kind of holiness that God evokes. Our knowledge of God is essential. No one will revere an immoral, uncaring, disinterested god. Those who heard Jesus pray this prayer were familiar with the Old Testament Scriptures. From those Scriptures they discovered that God is a God of justice, goodness, patience, and loving-kindness. These scriptures taught that what God has created is good and that God seeks to do good things for us. In Christ, the love of God is revealed more fully. We revere God not because God exists, but because God's holiness, goodness, justice, and love beckon our reverence.

Reverence is to believe that God is, to know God's character and nature, to be aware of God's presence, and to be willingly obedient and submissive to God's will. William Barclay tells us that "reverence is knowledge plus submission" (*The Gospel of St. Matthew* [Philadelphia: Westminster, 1956], 210). Therefore, Jesus could begin his prayer, "hallowed be your name." Jesus was very much aware of the third commandment and knew how essential it was for Israel. The holiness of God's name held everything together. If the people no longer had respect for the holiness of God, then community in general would decline. When God and God's name are honored, all life is sacred. When God is dishonored, nothing is sacred. A loss of reverence and respect for God's name causes us to lose respect and concern for one another. This is why God had Moses place the commandment for the respect and honoring of God's name near the top of the list in the Decalogue. Moses knew that respect and reverence for God's name lay at the root of all moral and spiritual values. Jesus understood this, so he set the phrase "hallowed be your name" at the beginning of his prayer.

> *If we lack reverence for God, how can we have reverence for one another and for the world around us?*

This part of the Lord's Prayer is extremely important for us for two reasons. First, if we lack reverence for God, how can we have reverence for one another and for the world around us? Reverence for God is the basis of our relationships. An absence of the sense of the "holy" causes life to decline.

The absence of the holy threatens our life together, disrupting community to the point that differences become divisive, resulting in the loss of respect and creating a sense of contempt. Sadly, this has happened to our urban communities, which are no longer safe for diversity. The loss of respect and reverence for human life creates a decline in relationships where friendship is replaced by a desire to gain personal control and advantage, where human nature is governed by greed, and where getting to know our neighbor is not seen as an opportunity for our highest good, but as a threat to our well-being.

> *The loss of the holy causes a decline in relationships where friendship is replaced by a desire to gain personal control and advantage.*

It is easy to tell when reverence is absent from relationships. When respect deteriorates, a person has no hesitation in using others for personal advantage or advancement. David, the king of Israel, treated Uriah in such a manner. David's desire for Bathsheba caused him to lose sight of respect and reverence for Uriah, Bathsheba's husband. So to David, Uriah became expendable. As his commander-in-chief, David placed Uriah in harm's way in order to cover up his affair with Bathsheba. When reverence, respect, and honor were lost, lust took over.

When reverence is absent, relationships become a means for personal convenience or advantage. People are no longer considered individuals with a sacredness of their own, but merely things to be used and manipulated. The lack of reverence leads to a lack of respect.

Not only is there disrespect for human life but for life in general as well, especially creation. Wendell Berry writes in his book *Christianity and the Survival of Creation* (New York: Pantheon-Random House, 1993) that the Bible does indeed instruct and command the Christian in the doctrines of sacredness of the earth and of all creation. Through the proper study of the Bible, Berry says, our destruction of nature is not merely bad stewardship or stupid economics or a betrayal of family responsibility; it is the most horrid blasphemy. It is flinging God's gifts into God's face, he declares, as of no worth beyond that assigned to them by our destruction of them. It appears that a disregard for the holy leads to a disregard and a disrespect for life in general.

Second, reverence for God is the basis for morality. If we lose sight of the holiness of God, nothing is holy. The third commandment, with its emphasis on reverence for God's name, was essential for community. It provided the cohesion for keeping the community together. Moses knew that a sense of the holy was essential not only to create community but also to keep it together and to build and maintain personal human relationships.

We hear a great deal today about the building of our infrastructure. It is a popular term. When we talk about rebuilding our infrastructure, we are referring to bridges, roads, railways, airports, and utilities. They have fallen into disrepair over the years, and are now desperately in need of repair. What about our moral infrastructure? What about our human relations and how we treat one another? Life appears to be out of control. How can we save it and rebuild it?

The St. Petersburg *Times* reported that in Florida fourteen adults were killed by youth ranging from fourteen to seventeen years of age in a single month in 1992. The article went on to point out that it was typical, not unusual, for that many homicides to be committed by youth in one month. There is a growing disregard for human life. When the holy, hallowed, and sacred are lost, violence takes over, causing and effecting little concern for human life. Our moral infrastructure is broken because God's name is not hallowed.

Most Americans were amazed to see the reaction of the people in England over the torture and murder of a two-year-old boy by two ten-year-old boys. Tens of thousands of people took to the streets in public outcry. Huge crowds gathered around the courthouse when the boys were being indicted. We were amazed because we never have seen any such response to the abuse or death of children in our country. It is so commonplace that it does not even make the front page. In Florida, as in other states, you can buy a speciality plate for your car. Some of these plates are designed with a picture of a panther with the inscription: "Save the Panther." The additional money that is collected through the sale of these plates goes to help preserve these animals from extinction. We need to place the face of a child on our license plates with the inscription "Save Our Children." They have become an endangered species. The disturbing, rising tide of violence is brought about by disrespect and the lack of reverence for human life. Communities cannot maintain sanity without some sense of the holy.

Further evidence for the demise of the holy is the loss of humility. Humility has received bad press in our day because it is associated with weakness. Anthony Bloom, in *A Guide for Prayer for Ministers and Other Servants* (Norman Shawchuck, ed. [Nashville: Upper Room, 1983]) points out that "humility" comes from the Latin word *humus,* meaning "fertile ground." "The fertile ground is there, unnoticed, taken for granted, always to be trodden upon. It is silent, inconspicuous, dark and yet it is always ready to receive any seed, ready to give it sustenance and life." He goes on to say, "The more lowly, the more fruitful, because it becomes really fertile when it accepts all the refuse of the earth. It is so low that nothing can soil it, abase it, humiliate it; it has accepted the last place and cannot go any lower" (p. 321). By accepting everything in such a miraculous way it transforms refuse into a power of life. Such is the power of humility. In simple terms, Richard Foster, in *Prayer,* defines *humility* as the means to live as close to the truth as possible—the truth about ourselves, the truth about others, and the truth about the world in which we live.

In a seminar, John Killinger commented on the subject of God's name as a hallowed name. He made the poignant statement that for Israel, the name of God was a "tent pole." It supported the whole framework. Then he went on to illustrate his point by referring to Robert E. Lee, whose name was great for many Americans. After the Civil War, Lee became president of Washington College, which later became Washington and Lee. During his days as college president he took trips down through Virginia, North Carolina, South Carolina, Georgia, and Florida. In small towns of no more than a few hundred people, thousands would come from miles around to gather at the train station, hoping to get a glimpse of Lee. Mothers would hold up their little boys, with notes in their hands informing Lee that they were named Robert E. Lee in honor of him. Killinger pointed out that the name of Robert E. Lee was a "tent pole" when the South needed a tent pole. The South was in despair, shame, and humiliation. Here was a man who carried himself straight and tall, of whom they were proud, giving them a sense of hope and dignity. If a human name can do so much, think of what God's name can do.

Moses stumbled unsuspectingly upon what proved to be a holy place. While he was keeping the flock of his father-in-law, Jethro, he came upon the burning bush. He arrived at this rendezvous with God as a result of the course of his duties as a shepherd. God called out to him from the bush, "Moses,

Moses, put off your shoes from your feet, for the place on which you are standing is holy ground." God got Moses' attention. Here at this holy place the soon to be liberator was liberated.

There must be some place in your life for the holy. Where is your holy ground? Where is your holy place, where God's name is "hallowed"? You need a place where God can tell you how much God loves you.

CHAPTER THREE

"Your kingdom come." (Matt. 6:10)

Marching to the Beat of a Different Drummer

I t has been suggested that the Lord's Prayer is mis-
named. It should be called the disciples' prayer. Jesus
taught this prayer to his disciples. William Barclay has
suggested that it is a prayer that only Jesus' disciples can
pray. It is the prayer of those who are part of the kingdom of
God—a prayer that sets the cadence for those who march to
the beat of a different drummer. It is a prayer for those in
the world but not of the world, living *under* secular govern-
ments and powers, but living *for* the principles and goals of
the kingdom of God.

A survey was conducted among laypersons to determine
their biggest complaint in regard to sermons. What do you
think they found out? The biggest complaint was the
preacher's use of words and jargon that people do not
understand—such words as *justification, sanctification,* and
judgment. Two women, as they were leaving church on a
Sunday morning, were discussing the preacher's sermon.
One woman was telling the other that she was convinced

their pastor was absolutely brilliant, "Because," she said, "I don't understand what he is talking about."

I would add one more word to that list of words not understood: *kingdom*. How much do you know about kingdoms? Few, if any of us, have ever lived under the rule of a king or a queen. But the people listening to Jesus understood such systems of government. When Jesus prayed, "Your kingdom come," the people understood what he meant by a kingdom. They lived under ruthless kings—especially Herod. Jesus' audience knew about despotism; vicious, cruel power; and tyranny. It was an everyday occurrence for them.

By this prayer, Jesus meant the opposite to the cruel reign of earthly kings. When his disciples prayed, they were praying for the reign of God, which would come with justice, righteousness, freedom, and love—the very opposite to the cruel and oppressive kings they knew. When the disciples prayed this prayer with all seriousness they were walking to the beat of a different drummer. They were throwing all caution to the wind, and they were not only praying for individuals but also for nations, not just for the coming of the kingdom but for the transformation of the world. The same is true for us. We pray for and work for the kingdom to come on earth—on all the earth—as it is in heaven.

In this prayer, we are saying, "Lord, allow human life to be what you intended it to be and break the stronghold of sin, oppression, and despair." Circumstances will not remain as they are, for God's kingdom will come on earth as it is in heaven, bringing change and transformation.

> *The kingdom of God is here, now.*

First, the kingdom of God is here, now. When Jesus was asked by the Pharisees when the kingdom of God was coming, he answered, "the kingdom of God is among you" (Luke 17:21). It has always been here. It will always be here as long as there are people who seek to do God's will. Like electricity, it has always been here. We did not invent electricity; we discovered it. It took Ben Franklin and his kite to create interest in it. It took Thomas Edison's ingenuity to bring it to us. The kingdom of God with its power, love, grace, peace, and hope has always been here. Jesus brought it close to us, closer to us than ever before, as close as flesh and blood. He demonstrated the kingdom of God in human life and encounter. It has always been here, but we have become the victims of the kingdom of darkness and despair—so much so that we have missed the meaning and hope offered by the kingdom of God.

A good illustration of how this could happen is seen by an incident in the life of Martin Niemöller. Niemöller was a German Lutheran pastor who led the resistance church movement against Hitler and Nazism in Germany prior to and during World War II. After the war, he was asked why the German people turned to Nazism. He replied that the Germans wanted something to bring their broken lives together, to provide coherence, meaning, and goals. He said that life was broken, at loose ends and fragmented. Hunger and poverty were rampant. The German people were in disgrace after the defeat of World War I, and Hitler offered them hope.

Nazism brought the German people together. It was an all-inclusive philosophy of life. For a while it seemed to be the answer to the unifying and rebuilding of Germany. But it was a false totalitarianism; it let them down. Niemöller said they were seeking the kingdom of God and did not know it. He said that they mistook Nazism for the real thing. Since our basic human need is to belong, disillusionment will come if we fail to seek God's will.

Second, this is a difficult part of the Lord's Prayer for us to pray. We are not sure what it means. We are hesitant because of the radical change that might take place if the prayer were answered.

Are we prepared for the radical change that this part of the Lord's Prayer will bring, both in our lives and our world? It will make a difference. When the kingdom comes, it will have a great impact on the way we make and spend money. For one thing, we would have a greater awareness of others and would give a more significant portion of what we possess to others. Jesus discussed the difference between those within and without the kingdom in the twenty-fifth chapter of Matthew. Those within the kingdom are given to generosity and hospitality. They will be those who gave food to the hungry, water to the thirsty, clothing to the naked, and shelter for the stranger. Jesus said that if anyone asks for your coat, you should give that person your cloak as well. If anyone asks you to walk a mile with him, go two miles. Such is the generosity of persons of the kingdom. Such generosity and self-giving will be the basis of God's final judgment (Matt. 25:31-46).

> *If we really prayed for the kingdom to come, we would seek out any persons we may have abused or misused and ask their forgiveness.*

If we really prayed for the kingdom to come, we will seek out any persons we may have abused or misused and ask their forgiveness. Businesspersons who pray this prayer will reform their business practices. They will provide better value for their customers and care more for their employees and their families. They will avoid discriminatory hiring practices. A politician who prays this prayer will make good his or her campaign promises. A physician who prays this prayer will be consumed by a compassion to heal. Everyone who prays this prayer will give a greater place to honor than to honoraria. When we pray this prayer, we will march to the beat of a different drummer. Jesus, in the Sermon on the Mount, best describes those who seek to live within the kingdom. The poor in spirit, the meek, and the humble will inherit the kingdom rather than the arrogant and the selfish. Peacemakers will be the children of God. The members of the kingdom are those who are persecuted for their commitment to righteousness, goodness, and love.

If you pray this prayer, you are praying for a kingdom to come upon the earth that will radically transform human life. Life in the world is dominated by greed, self-centeredness, pride, and arrogance. It is out of step with the kingdom of God. Within the kingdom, faith, hope, and love abide. To pray "Your kingdom come. Your will be done, on earth as it is in heaven" is to march to the beat of a different drummer. The apostle Paul admonishes us "not be conformed to this world, but be transformed by the renewing of your minds, so that you may discern what is the will of God—what is good and acceptable and perfect" (Rom. 12:2).

Ours is a power-oriented world—institutional power, political power, economic and corporate power, as well as personal power. If we seriously pray for this part of the Lord's Prayer to take place in our lives, we must come to grips with our use of power. If God's kingdom is to prevail in our lives, the way we use power becomes a critical issue.

I have always considered Jesus' temptation in Luke 4 as a struggle with power. How would Jesus use his power? This question is raised right at the beginning of his public ministry, right on the heels of his baptism. In the wilderness experience, Jesus was tempted to use his power for himself.

He was tempted to turn the stones into bread for food to satisfy his own hunger. Jesus realized he was being tempted to use his power to obtain food in a manner that other men and women could not. Without hesitation, he rejected this use of power. When he did perform a miracle in regard to bread, it was to feed hungry people. Certainly this event set the tone for the kingdom of God on earth.

The coming of the kingdom into our lives challenges us to resolve the issue of how we use power. Each of us, to some degree, exerts personal influence and power. We are tempted to use it for our advantage. This can happen in our work relationships or at home in our personal relationships. What about those "power plays" we make with our colleagues, spouses, and children? We are tempted to take advantage of others because of our position of privilege. The Bible considers it a grievous sin to take advantage of another person by misusing our position of power and influence. Jesus had more problems with the religious leaders of his day who used their power for selfish purposes than with any other group of people. In practical terms, it is a grievous sin to take advantage of the elderly because of our youth, to take advantage of the weak because of our strength, to take advantage of the poor because of our wealth, or to take advantage of a lesser employee because of our seniority or status. Do you get the picture? How great is the temptation to misuse what God has given to us for personal advantage.

> *We are tempted to take advantage of others because of our position of privilege.*

To be a faithful member of the kingdom of God, Jesus points out to us, we are to

Love your enemies, do good to those who hate you, bless those who curse you, pray for those who abuse you. If anyone strikes you on the cheek, offer the other also; and from anyone who takes away your coat do not withhold even your shirt. Give to everyone who begs from you; and if anyone takes away your goods, do not ask for them again. Do to others as you would have them do to you. (Luke 6:27-31 NRSV)

When we are tempted to use our talents, gifts, and special powers for ourselves we are then falling into the trap that caught the medieval church, which felt that what it did in the church was more important than what it did in the world. It is heresy for the church to think that it is the object of its own mission. The Lord's Prayer is dangerous for anyone to pray who practices a selfish and abusive use of power—dangerous in the sense that one cannot pray this part of the Lord's Prayer and remain the same.

Think of the many Christians from the first century until the present who have committed their lives to the kingdom of God but have seen very little evidence of the kingdom in their lifetime. We may not see much evidence of that kingdom, but we can march to the beat of the kingdom. Moses was called by God to lead his people from slavery to the promised land, but Moses never got there. There was a regrettable moment in his life, a moment of weakness that cost him the promised land. He could see the land only from a distance. At the time of Moses' death, God took him to the plains of Moab to Mount Nebo. There the Lord showed him all the land that had been promised to Abraham. And the Lord said to Moses, "I have let you see it with your eyes, but you shall not cross over there." Although Moses never got to the promised land, he walked and talked like a man who was on his way there.

We may never see the day when the fullness of the kingdom of God comes on the earth. But we pray for the kingdom's coming. We must walk and talk like people who are on their way to the kingdom. We must not march to the cadence of the kingdoms of this world, but as the followers of Jesus Christ, who are bound for the promised land—we march to the beat of a different drummer.

CHAPTER FOUR

> *"Your will be done." (Matt. 6:10).*

A Risky and Dangerous Prayer

The question is not whether we are succeeding or failing but whether we are doing the will of God. Nothing is as joyful or stimulating as success. But such joy is very deceptive if it comes from the satisfaction of an ambition that is contrary to the will of God. Failure is always painful, but the pain is fruitful if it is part of God's purpose. A failure within the purpose of God is no longer a failure. In the cross, Jesus met the horror of failure, because his disciples deserted him. His enemies, whom he

> *A failure within the purpose of God is no longer a failure.*

sought to save, crucified him. He experienced insults, torture, the sensation of having been abandoned by God, and finally death as a common criminal on a despised cross. By all human standards his life to this point had been a dismal failure. When it comes to the will and purpose of God, it is not possible to establish a clear-cut distinction between success and failure—at least, not by what the world has determined as success. The will of God and the kingdom of God are related in the Lord's Prayer. The kingdom of God will come when the will of God is done. Here Jesus talks about the will of God being done on earth as fully and perfectly as it is in heaven. This, in a sense, is the radical will of God, which will be fully done when God's kingdom is fully come. But it also represents God's will for us in this present order. Even the most difficult sayings of the Sermon on the Mount, of which the Lord's Prayer is a part, serve the important function of making us aware of the perfect will of God, whether we are capable of doing it or not. If we cannot perform the perfect will of God, we can nevertheless be transformed by it. For Jesus, the standard for human conduct is the eternal will of God, not human ability. When men and women through faith are able to fulfill the will of God, the kingdom of God will come among them.

> *For Jesus, the standard for human conduct is the eternal will of God, not human ability.*

Jesus clearly connects the kingdom of God and the will of God. What God wills in heaven is to be done on earth. Therefore, the demand of the kingdom of God for us here and now is this: Let what God wills be done. This was true for Jesus in his passion and personal struggle in Gethsemane, "not my will but thine be done." Jesus defines his task and purpose in John 4:34; 5:30: "My food is to do the will of him who sent me . . . because I seek to do not my own will but the will of him who sent me." This is true for his followers as well, as Jesus clearly points out, "Whoever does the will of God is my brother and sister and mother" (Mark 3:35). Again Jesus declared, "Not everyone who says to me, 'Lord, Lord,' will enter the kingdom of heaven, but only the one who does the will of my Father in heaven" (Matt. 7:21). There is no doubt, and it is confirmed throughout the entire New Testament, that the supreme norm is "the will of God."

The will of God involves struggle, and this struggle involves agony, loneliness, trust, and courage. Jesus' personal struggle with the will of God involves agony. The agony for him is in the cross and death. No one wants to die, especially at the age of thirty-three—least of all to die the agonizing death on the cross. For Jesus, the struggle in Gethsemane involves his knowledge of God's will and his struggle to accept it. It is agony because the will of God is taking his life in a direction that he does not want to go. Before him looms the cross. Jesus knows all too well the reality of the cross—crucifixion and death.

Thus this part of the Lord's Prayer can be dangerous. The will of God can lead us in a direction or to a place that we are not willing to go. It may lead us into an experience we do not want to face. It could cause us to meet people we really do not want to meet. The agony is bringing our will in line with the will of God.

Decision making often involves pain and agony, because it causes us to struggle with alternatives. The important decisions in our lives are not made without a struggle. When it comes to the will of God, we do have a choice. We can accept or reject it. This is Jesus' dilemma in the garden. He agonizes over the choice he is to make, whether to submit or to resist the will of God. Barclay reminds us that "every person has his private Gethsemane, and every person has to learn to say, 'Thy will be done.' "

The agony in this struggle is intensified by the lack of knowledge. It is in such experience that our faith is tried to its utmost limits, because our submission to God's will does not bring to us the full knowledge or understanding of what lies ahead. How many times have we said, "Had I known then what I know now I would never have begun such a journey or undertaken such a task." To pray for God's will "to come on earth as it is in heaven" could produce an agonizing experience for all involved. To bring our world, our behavior, our actions, and our desires in line with the will of God certainly will bring about agonizing, painful changes in our lives.

> *The struggle over the will of God could be a lonely experience.*

The struggle over the will of God could be a lonely experience. In Gethsemane, Jesus left his friends and faced his struggle alone. Even though the Lord's Prayer leads us to pray for the will of God to come on earth, yet it remains the personal struggle of each person. The hymn writer reminds us that this is when "other helpers fail and comforts flee." The struggle over the will of God is a very lonely struggle, because no one can do it for you. No one can submit to the will of God on your behalf. Bishop Fulton Sheen was asked to pray before the New York State Legislature. He replied to the invitation by saying, "I am not going to pray for you. There are certain things that you need to do for yourself. You need to blow your own nose, make your own love, and say your own prayers." The prayerful struggle to ascertain the will of God is a personal and often lonely struggle that each one must endure.

The struggle over the will of God involves trust and courage. Think of all those men and women who were convinced that the will of God meant that all should be free from tyranny and bondage. Their struggle to accomplish the will of God involved the deepest trust and courage. Who of us is not inspired by the trust and courage exemplified by Archbishop Oscar Romero of El Salvador, who sought to bring freedom for his people amid the political corruption, sadistic violence, and economic exploitation in his country? For Archbishop Romero this was, without a doubt, the will of God. He realized that by his own submission to the will of God through Christ and by risking his own life could the liberty and resurrection power of God come to his people. Nothing could be more potently symbolic than the fact that Archbishop Romero was gunned down by his opponents while saying mass.

Our prayer for God's will to be done on earth as it is in heaven may involve a great deal of trust and courage on our part, because we are not totally certain where such a prayer will lead us. In such a prayerful moment it is possible for us to know something of heaven that we may face the battles of earth.

How can we know the will of God? How can we know that we are doing the will of God? I have been asked that question more times than perhaps any other question. Several factors provide guidance for us at this point. The most obvious and basic factor is tested by the standards established in the life and teachings of Jesus. Anything that we are tempted to do that is inconsistent with the life and teachings of Jesus is not of God. Anything that is contrary to Jesus' example is not God's will.

Long before the revelation of Jesus, it was David's practice to put on the ephod of God in times of struggle and confusion. The ephod was symbolic of God's presence, much as the Ark of the Covenant. David wore the ephod as a warrior when he was entering battle so that he would know the will of God as he sought to engage the enemy.

Today we do not have an ephod or any physical garment to remind us what the will of God is. But we do have a source of guidance. We have the Holy Spirit to help us understand the will of God. Jesus told us that the Holy Spirit would lead us into all truth. The people of Israel were guided by a pillar of fire by night and a cloud by day, and the ephod symbolized God's presence. Today, the Holy Spirit is present not only to lead us into the knowledge of God's will but to empower us to perform the will of God as well.

Much pain and suffering has come upon people's lives from those who were convinced that they were doing the will of God. One painful and obvious illustration is the Crusades during the Middle Ages. Warriors were convinced that God had called them to rescue from Islamic rule the Holy Land in Palestine, especially Jerusalem. The four hundred years of the Crusades is one of the saddest periods in the history of the Christian church. All kinds of atrocities and brutality were done in the name of God, because those directing the Crusades were convinced that it was the will of God. It was also one of the worst periods of anti-Semitism in the history of the church, and done as the will of God. Kenneth Scott Latourette, a church historian, points out that the Crusades were an effort to achieve the kingdom of God on earth by the methods of that world that the New Testament declares to be at enmity with the gospel. The Crusades constituted a complete reversal of the attitude of the early Christians toward war, which was one predominantly of condemnation (*History of Christianity*, pp. 408ff.). From this developed the idea that wars could be "just." From then until now, some wars have been regarded "holy," in fulfillment of the purposes of God. In a reversal of prevailing attitudes in the apostolic church, the phrase *Deus vult* ("God wills it") became the battle cry.

Think of the pain and suffering that are still perpetrated in our world by those who seek to practice ethnic and racial cleansing, convinced that they are doing the will of God. People feel vindicated for their actions because what they do is done as "the will of God." Harry Emerson Fosdick quotes a seventeenth-century secularist as saying, "I had rather meet coming against me a whole regiment with drawn swords than one Calvinist convinced that he is doing the will of God" (*Great Voices of the Reformation* [New York: Random House, 1952], 201).

But what is it that God wills? From the first to the last pages of the Bible, it is clear that God's will is our well-being at all levels; that God's will is a helpful, healing, liberating, and saving will. God wills life, joy, freedom, peace, and happiness—for both the individual and humankind. This is the meaning of God's absolute future, God's victory, and God's kingdom, which Jesus proclaimed—bringing liberation, salvation, satisfaction, and joy. God wills nothing but human well-being.

It is impossible to fully know the will of God without knowing the story of Jesus Christ. Saul of Tarsus thought that he knew the will of God. Therefore, in defending the faith of his ancestors, he brought persecution and havoc against the early Christian church. He was convinced that this radical movement of Christians was working against the will and purpose of the God of Israel. He did all that he could to stop it, convinced that his actions were the will of God. He was protecting the faith. What an honorable task he felt he had undertaken. It was not until his dramatic encounter with Jesus on the road to Damascus that he discovered why he had it all wrong. All of this time he had actually been working against God's will and purpose in human life. Because of his experience of persecuting Christians, Paul always considered himself the "least of all the apostles." The same is true for all of us: The fullness of God's will is to be found only in Jesus Christ.

Nevertheless, this remains a very difficult portion of the Lord's Prayer for us to pray. To take it seriously would bring about radical change. I am not sure we want that kind of change. There are those who want a carefree life undaunted by moral restraints. A serious consideration of God's will for one's life would seriously cramp the lifestyle of many people. I am grateful to John Baillie for his prayer regarding the will of God:

In Thy will, O Lord, is my peace.
In Thy love is my rest.
In Thy service is my joy.
Thou art all my heart's desire.
Whom have I in heaven but Thee?
And there is none upon earth that I desire besides Thee.
(John Baillie, *A Diary of Private Prayer*)

It is dangerous and risky to pray, "your kingdom come, your will be done." Jesus is not suggesting that this new life in the kingdom means putting new wine into old wineskins, or a new patch on an old garment. Here we are faced with something new, and it is going to be dangerous to the old.

CHAPTER FIVE

"*Give us this day our daily bread.*" (*Matt. 6:11*)

Bread for the Journey

o we really take this part of the Lord's Prayer seriously? What sense does it make for a company of people who are so well fed to pray such a prayer? How can a group of people who go shopping once a week and fill their refrigerators and freezers with enough food for weeks pray such a prayer with meaning? How is it possible to push your cart through a supermarket with mounds of fresh vegetables, breads, and meats and then to pray a prayer for God to provide daily bread? What sense does it make for a group of people for whom not the lack of food but too much food is a problem, who spend enormous amounts of money on diets and diet foods to lose weight, to engage in this part of the Lord's Prayer? Doesn't it appear awkward for such people to come together once a week and repeat a prayer that contains the request "Give us this day our daily bread"? Does this portion of the Lord's Prayer have any relevance or meaning for us?

We need to face the fact that wealthy Christians are not living under the same conditions as the people to whom Jesus first taught these words. We are not Palestinian peasants who are tilling our strip of ground and anxiously waiting each year for the harvest on which our very existence depends. The people to whom Jesus was speaking were a heartbeat away from starvation. Starving and hungry people think of little else besides daily bread. This was their desperate, all-consuming, pressing, daily need, so they paid attention to the Lord's Prayer. These words had special meaning for them.

David H. C. Read, before he became pastor of Madison Avenue Presbyterian Church in New York, served as an officer in the British Army during World War II. During the summer of 1942, he was enjoying an evening meal in an exquisite restaurant in Normandy. Ten days later he was captured by the Germans and was held prisoner of war. He was literally begging for bread. For the next two years, he shared one loaf of bread a day with eight other men. The plea "Give us this day our daily bread" took on new meaning for him. Read said he became aware of how thin the curtain is of our modern civilization. How precarious is the affluence that we take for granted. How quickly it can all change. The people in south Florida discovered that life can change within just a few minutes. Because of Hurricane Andrew's powerful winds, suddenly and without notice, the words *bread* and *water* took on a new meaning. The people of the San Fernando Valley in California understand what it means to line up for food stamps and water after one minute of earth-shattering terror. How can we forget that at this very moment millions, perhaps one third of the world's population, are in need of their daily supply of rice and bread? It is the basic gnawing need of their lives. When we pray this part of the Lord's Prayer, we must not lose sight of the word *our*. In this prayer we are joining in the cry and need of the human family to which we belong; we are praying not only for ourselves but for all the people on earth.

We pray for our daily bread because it reveals to us that God is concerned with our pressing daily needs, whatever those needs may be. To those who heard this prayer in the first century, the vital need was bread, and that need was God's concern. Your need today may not be for bread, but it could be just as critical and life threatening. This part of the Lord's Prayer is about more than bread; it is whatever our daily need may be. We can be sure that it is of concern to God. Do not hide it, but reveal your need to God in prayer. If anything is worth worrying about, it is worth praying about.

> *This part of the Lord's Prayer is about more than bread; it is whatever our daily need may be.*

God is concerned about our daily needs, regardless of how trivial they may seem to us. Jesus went to the wedding in Cana of Galilee because he enjoyed being with people, and he looked forward to a joyous occasion. It was a time of joyous merrymaking, and Jesus wanted to be part of it. On such occasions Jesus took his food with gladness.

It was in the midst of this joyous festivity that the worst possible thing happened: They ran out of wine. For a Jewish feast, wine was essential. In the East, showing hospitality was a sacred duty, and for the provisions to fail at a wedding would have been a terrible embarrassment to the bride and the groom. Jesus was concerned about the embarrassment this occasion created and the potential social disgrace that would be experienced by the bride's family.

So Jesus produced an abundance of wine for the occasion. This was the opening event of John's Gospel in regard to Jesus' ministry. For John, this event was a sign that revealed the compassion and concern that Jesus had for people in critical circumstances. It happened in an out-of-the-way village, to a humble, poor family. There were no crowds! It did not draw the attention of others. On Jesus' part it was a deep, sensitive concern for human need. When we pray, "Give us this day our daily bread," we are praying to a God who is concerned with our need, a God who goes out of the way to find the poor, the sick, and the powerless.

It is fully in order for us to pray for "our daily bread." By this phrase Jesus has transformed the trivialities of everyday life. How difficult life would be if we were forbidden to pray for the common, ordinary and little things, because they make up the bulk of life. When we pray for "our daily bread," we know that God is not only concerned that we have enough food on our tables, but also whether there is medicine for the sick child, whether there is money to pay the bills, whether the children are failing in school, whether Dad has lost his job, whether a brother or sister has been humiliated. All of this is the substance of our prayer, "Give us this day our daily bread."

We pray for our daily bread because bread is the gift of God. It reveals our dependence on God. It is God who gives the wheat. No person has created a seed that will grow. All loving things come from God. It is God who provides the grain, and through human cooperation the seed is sown, watered, and harvested. Then it is ground to flour, baked, and enjoyed. Our food is a direct gift from God. Our prayer for "our daily bread" acknowledges that the seed, the flour, and the bread are the results of God's activity and goodness.

A good illustration of God's providence is what happened to the Israelites regarding the manna in the wilderness. Manna was life-giving bread given by God to the Israelites as they journeyed from Egypt to the promised land. God provided this breadlike substance, which tasted like wafers made with honey, to keep them alive. Thus God provided bread for the journey. Every morning when they awoke, they found manna on the ground. They were to collect only what they could eat that day. If they became greedy and gathered more than they needed for a single day, it became infested with worms. They learned that every day God would provide them with food for their journey to the promised land. If they trusted God for their daily bread and took no more than a daily supply, then God would provide for them. This giving of the manna reveals how, through faith and confidence, "food" abounds, even in the "wilderness."

Terence Fretheim, in his commentary *Exodus*, points out how important it is to stress the naturalness of the manna: "It is precisely the 'natural' that is seen as a gift of God" (p. 181). It was the gift of creation that was placed at Israel's disposal, although it appeared to them as miraculous. Fretheim states that by viewing God's provisions in the wilderness, or in times of crisis, as miraculous and extraordinary, we tend to view God's concerns for our daily needs outside the realm of the ordinary. The result is that God is removed from the ordinary and everyday happenings and we go searching for God in those mountaintop experiences; the prayer for daily bread loses its significance. If we fail to see God in the ordinary, everyday experiences of daily bread, and if the miraculous is excluded from daily life, the result will be the absence of God altogether.

How many times does the crisis of a daily need or physical suffering create a crisis of faith? Our material and spiritual well-being are more closely linked than we would like to admit. It appears that Israel's mind was so clouded by the lack of daily food that the presence of God in their everyday lives became obscure and distant.

> *Our material and spiritual well-being are more closely linked than we would like to admit.*

Both Moses' admonition to Israel and Jesus' emphasis on praying for our daily bread focus on the presence of God in connection with our daily needs. Certainly Moses' task in this manna narrative is to get the Israelites to confess that God is the one who has brought them out of the bondage of Egypt, in a most dramatic fashion, but not to lose sight of the divine factor in every daily blessing of life. Therefore, not only do we pray for our daily bread, but we give thanks for it as well. Moses instructed the people clearly: This bread is from God. Fretheim points out:

> The divine activity on behalf of the people is not focused simply on the dramatic moments in their lives. God is concerned about all the little things that go to make up their daily rounds. God is a factor to be reckoned with everywhere, in everything, even the natural process of the daily order. God is the one who cares for them in such a way as to respond to their prayers for daily bread. The people of God do not live by bread alone, but they cannot live without bread either. (*Exodus*, p. 184)

The word *daily* is the key to this part of the prayer. We are praying for the needs of this coming day. Our concerns are for our children, jobs, health, responsibilities, and the struggle of relationships at home and work. We pray for patience, wisdom, and compassion—daily, hourly. Such daily prayer is not for extravagance or luxury, but for day-to-day provisions, for day-to-day survival. To pray for daily bread is to take one day at a time.

This portion of the Lord's Prayer suggests that the gathering of provisions is for only one day at a time. The will of God is a "discipline of dailiness." There is to be no hoarding of the gifts of God's creation, no tearing down of barns and the building of greater ones, no anxiety about what we are to eat tomorrow. The issue becomes one of learning to depend on God for our daily needs, "for where your treasure is, there your heart will be also" (Luke 12:34).

The manna was a symbol of the people's dependence on God as they marched through the wilderness to the promised land. Jesus was aware of this incident, and it adds to our understanding of the Lord's Prayer and the request for "daily bread." Jesus alluded to this in his prayer; we are to trust the Father as we march through the wilderness to the promised land. God provides bread for the journey. In this portion of the Lord's Prayer we are saying, "O Lord, not only is our life from you, but what we need to sustain our life, our daily bread, is from you."

At the Sea of Galilee, Jesus told the masses, "I am the bread of life. Whoever comes to me will never be hungry, and whoever believes in me will never be thirsty" (John 6:35). Bread is essential for life. It sustains life, and life cannot go on without it. Jesus brings to us the fullness of life. He is essential to life—in essence, the bread of life. In him all of our unsatisfied longings, all of our insatiable desires of the heart are fulfilled. In Christ, the bread of life, the restless soul is at rest, the hunger is sated, the thirst for life is quenched. This bread of life, for the journey of life, is ours for the taking, for the asking.

CHAPTER SIX

Forgiven–Forgiving

Simon Wiesenthal survived the Nazi concentration camps where eighty-nine members of his family perished. He wrote the book *The Sunflower*, which begins with a haunting story that took place during his imprisonment. He was selected at random from a work detail, yanked aside, and taken up the back stairs to a hospital corridor where a nurse led him into a dark room. He was left alone in that dark hospital room with a pitiful figure wrapped in white, lying on a bed. The man was a German officer who had been badly wounded. Parts of his body were covered with yellow-stained bandages, and gauze covered his entire face.

In a weak, trembling voice the man offered a sacramental confession to Wiesenthal. He recounted his earlier years, telling about his days in Hitler's youth movement. He told Wiesenthal about his actions on the Russian front and the harsh treatment that was wrought against the Jews by his SS unit. Then he told of a horrible atrocity, when his unit herded all the Jews in one town into a wooden building and torched it. He told how some of the Jews with their clothing ablaze leaped from the second story and the SS troops, he among them, shot them as they fell. He started to tell Wiesenthal about one boy with dark eyes and hair, but his voice gave way.

Several times Wiesenthal tried to leave the room, but each time the mummy-like figure would reach out with his cold, bloodless hand and restrain him from leaving. Finally, after several hours, the German officer explained why he had summoned a Jewish prisoner to his bedside. "I know what I am asking is almost too much for you. But without your answer I cannot die in peace." Then he asked Wiesenthal for forgiveness for all of his crimes against the Jews. He was asking a Jewish prisoner, who might die next at the hands of his SS comrades, to forgive him.

Wiesenthal stood in silence for some time, staring at the man's bandaged face. Then he made up his mind and left the room without saying a word. He left the soldier to die unforgiven. Who among us could pass judgment on such an unbearable dilemma that confronted Wiesenthal in that hospital room?

But the Bible adds an interesting twist to one aspect of the dilemma that he faced. It records an incident in the life of a thirty-three-year-old man, an itinerant preacher from Nazareth. He healed the sick, fed the hungry, befriended the leper, the poor, and the forgotten people. His name was Jesus of Nazareth, and he taught the masses the meaning of love and forgiveness. The authorities sought to silence him, so they condemned him to die on a cross. His tormentors, accusers, and those performing his execution gathered to watch him die.

The crowd was made up of those who drove the nails into his palms, pierced his side with a sword, and placed a crown of thorns on his brow and mockingly called him the "King of the Jews." He looked down at those who cried out for his crucifixion, who gambled for his sole possession, a seamless robe, who mocked and ridiculed him with anger and death in their eyes and said, "Father, forgive them for they do not know what they are doing." As Simon Wiesenthal's story reveals, of all the acts that Jesus performed, this is the hardest for us to practice—forgiving those who have sinned against us. A literal translation of this part of the Lord's Prayer is

"Forgive us our sins, in proportion as we forgive those who have sinned against us."

To make sure we understand this, Jesus gives us a commentary on this portion of the Lord's Prayer in the verses that follow. In simple language, God's forgiveness is related to our forgiveness of others. This prayer is a conditional request—we are forgiven as we forgive.

> *In simple language, God's forgiveness is related to our forgiveness of others.*

In the affairs of human beings, there is a vicious cycle of retaliation. You gore my ox, and I will gore your ox. You hurt me, and I'll hurt you. You strike me, and I'll strike you. You kill my people, and I'll kill your people. It keeps the world on edge, divided, and fragmented in a constant state of strife.

> *Forgiveness is important because it breaks the law of retaliation.*

Richard Foster reminds us that:

as long as the only cry heard among us is for vengeance, there can be no reconciliation. If our hearts are so narrow as to see only how others have hurt and offended us, we cannot see how we have offended God and so find no need to seek forgiveness. If we are always calculating in our hearts how much this one or that one has violated our rights, by the very nature of things we will not be able to pray this prayer. (*Prayer*, p. 187)

Forgiveness is important because it breaks the law of retaliation. When offended, instead of offending in return, we forgive. Why? We can do this only because of the supreme act of forgiveness from Jesus on the cross. Here, once and for all, the back of retaliation is broken. Forgiveness releases a flood tide of forgiving graces among people.

If forgiveness is so important, what is forgiveness? How do we define it? First of all, let me say what forgiveness is not. It does not mean that we cease to hurt. Some wounds that we suffer are deep, and they may hurt for a long time. And the fact that we continue in the anguish of emotional pain does not mean that we have failed to forgive.

We have often heard the phrase "to forgive and to forget." There are some things, especially a traumatic experience, that we will never forget. It is impossible to forget, but in forgiving we no longer allow the memory to be used against others.

> *Forgiveness is not unconditional. It assumes repentance on the part of the one who is praying for forgiveness.*

We are kidding ourselves if we say that the incident really did not matter. It did matter, and it does matter. There is no use pretending otherwise. But in forgiving we no longer allow the offense to control and dominate our behavior.

It is foolish on our part to try to convince ourselves that things will be just as they were before. Things will never be the same. By the grace of God they will be a lot better, but they will never be the same.

Forgiveness is not unconditional. It assumes repentance on the part of the one who is praying for forgiveness. There is nothing to be gained by a man who has beaten his wife in a drunken rage if he has no intention of dealing with his alcohol problem. The Lord's Prayer, along with the commentary attached in Matthew 6:14-15, does not suggest that God's forgiveness is given out in the number of times we have forgiven. Rather, we must genuinely repent of our hardness of heart before expecting to receive God's mercy and forgiveness.

Forgiveness is not something that is earned. It would be foolish for us to believe that we can earn God's forgiveness by forgiving others. Conversely, it would be foolish for us to conclude that God is incapable of forgiving our sin of unwillingness, which refuses to forgive someone who has hurt us deeply. The parable told by Jesus in Matthew 18:22-35 solemnly warns us that we must fervently pray for strength to resist the temptation of getting even with those who have hurt us and for grace to offer sincere forgiveness.

Douglas Hare, in his commentary *Matthew*, points out that unlimited forgiveness is not to be confused with sentimental toleration of hurtful behavior:

> Christians are often guilty of forgiving too much too quickly. The misbehavior of alcoholics is not to be laughed off. Ministers who fail to control their sexual impulses are not to be lightly excused. Teenagers who betray their parents' trust are not simply to be forgiven; a much more loving course of action is to insist that they amend their behavior so that they can regain that trust. In these and other instances premature forgiveness is an easy way out that does little to help the offender or to heal a damaged relationship. (*Matthew*, p. 218)

What is forgiveness? Richard Foster defines it as the miracle of grace. If a husband ignores his wife, valuing business, career, and other things ahead of her, he has sinned against her. The offense is real, and the hurt is deep. A sacred trust has been broken. A wedge has come between them, forcing

63

them apart. The wife will never forget the violation of trust and respect. Even in her old age she may feel the icy chill at the memory of her husband's disregard of her.

But forgiveness means that this horrible offense will not separate them. Forgiveness means that the power of love and reconciling grace that holds them together is greater than the power of the offense that separates them. This is forgiveness.

To pray "forgive us our sins" is most certainly needed, and how desperate and sick we are until we find it. Here is a man who ruined his children's lives. He made a botch of things. Now he cannot get it out of his mind. It haunts him even in the middle of the night. Here is a woman who failed a friend. She did not have the strength to share with her when she so desperately needed it. Her friend committed suicide. How can she ever forgive herself? Here is an adolescent girl whose parents loved her with every ounce of their being. She was surrounded with love and care. The girl is now a junkie and living on the streets. She has only begun to realize what she has done, not only to herself but to her parents as well. How will she be able to bear it?

How wonderful it is to experience forgiveness, to know down deep in your soul that the past is covered over and the future can be pure and good. Is not this the theme of Charles Wesley's hymn?

> He breaks the power of canceled sin,
> He sets the prisoner free,
> his blood can make the foulest clean,
> his blood availed for me.

Leslie Weatherhead reminds us that the forgiveness of sins is the most therapeutic idea in the world. If you really believe that God has forgiven you, then the burden of guilt and the fear at the heart of it will disappear. Weatherhead concludes that "if this great idea is really received by the mind, not only by the intellect, but by the emotions as well, then it is like the dawn breaking after a long night of black torture" (*Psychology, Religion, and Healing* [Nashville: Abingdon Press, 1951], 334).

I read recently the story of a twelve-year-old boy in California who had witnessed the brutal murder of his mother and father. His life appeared ruined. He was sent to a state school for boys and became apathetic and withdrawn. He was doing poorly in his classes. Neither a psychologist nor a therapist could penetrate the shield of defenses that his mind had thrown up.

After graduating from high school, he attend a Young Life meeting. It was here that he heard a youth testify about the difference Christ had made in his life. After this experience, he became a Christian, and his entire life was turned around. Where he had been introverted and withdrawn, he now began to make new friends.

He went on to law school, and there he did something he had wanted to do since the time of his conversion: He visited the man who had killed his parents. The man was serving a life sentence in the state penitentiary. Their first visit was not good; they both were nervous, and it was difficult for them to talk to each other. However, he continued to go back for visits, and finally there was a breakthrough. The young man told the prisoner, "If God can forgive me for the awful hatred I carried for you, God can forgive you for what you have done."

A few years later, the prisoner was paroled. The young man was now an attorney in Modesto, California. He helped the now former prisoner get a job and start a new life. This story may be incredible and unbelievable, but it is about the power of Christ and forgiveness. That is what it means to pray, "Forgive us our sins, as we forgive those who sin against us."

CHAPTER SEVEN

> *"And do not bring us to the time of trial."*
> *(Matt. 6:13)*

A Place to Stand

In today's world, most of our presumptions have been challenged. For many persons, the temptations and challenges of our modern world have been too much. The key to our faith lies in finding a firm place from which to operate. It was Archimedes who said, "Give me a place to stand and I will move the earth." His contemporaries felt that Archimedes had accomplished wonders. His response to them was that "the fulcrum has to be firm." As we face the onslaught of temptation, our fulcrum needs to be firm. We need a place to stand.

For most people, this is probably the most disturbing portion of the Lord's Prayer. How can we ask God to keep us from temptation? This appears impossible and seems contradictory to life, because temptation seems to come with being human. Life is a constant struggle with temptation. But asking God to keep us from life's struggle and decisions is like asking God to keep us from being human.

We are always under the attack of temptation. Martin Luther, when discussing temptation, said, "We cannot keep the birds from flying over our heads, but we can keep them from making a nest in our hair." We can sense the despair of the person who said, "I can resist anything but temptation."

Too often we think of temptation as a bad word, that it is something that seeks to seduce us into evil. The biblical word for "temptation" is better translated "to test" rather than "to seduce." The purpose of temptation is to test one's strength, loyalty, and ability for service.

If steel is to be used for engineering purposes it has to pass a stress test. This test is quite stringent, especially if the steel is to be used in a bridge or a high-rise building. Recently an overpass on one of our interstate highways collapsed. Repair workers discovered that the steel used in the overpass was not sufficient to bear the traffic load. How many times have we faltered under the burden of stress, because we did not have sufficient emotional or spiritual strength or stamina?

Abraham was commanded by God to take his son Isaac to Mt. Moriah to offer him as a burnt offering upon the mountain. In this experience, Abraham discovered that God was both the tester and the provider. This testing of Abraham by God was to determine whether Abraham would trust only God or if we would at the same time look to other gods.

Temptation comes from numerous directions. The attack may come from outside of us. Certain people present a bad influence, in whose presence it is easy for us to do the wrong thing. There are certain environments where unscrupulous behavior would never be questioned or challenged. We may have associations and friendships that do not add to the nobler and finer things of life.

> *The temptation from outside is the temptation to despair.*

The temptation from outside is the temptation to despair. We live in a period of remarkable human accomplishment, especially in regard to technology. There seems to be no limit to human ingenuity. What humans set their minds to do, they do! Three decades ago we set our minds on getting to the moon, and we did it. One cannot fail to be impressed by the skill required in placing men and women in orbit, but today it has become commonplace. At the same time, our moral failure has brought a feeling of deep despair. This despair is reflected in a bumper sticker I saw recently: "I feel so much better since I have given up hope." Today's failure stems from our inability to put our "biggest minds" on our "biggest problems." We are tempted to believe that all the answers lie in technology.

The reason why we are tempted to despair results from confusion. People simply do not know what to think or in whom to believe and trust. This has resulted in bitter disappointment. The civil rights struggles of the 1950s and 1960s seemed to offer some hope for racial justice. Today that hope has been diminished. Technology that was to bring Utopia has brought suffocating human problems instead. Jacques Ellul, in his book *The Technological Society,* points out how technology has created "artificiality" in its opposition to nature. The world that is tempted to put all its eggs in the technological basket is creating, in Ellul's words, "an artificial world that is radically different from the natural world." He points out that technology has created a tale of the human whose intelligence has been subordinated to a machine, a procedure, a system, and a program. It is the tale of the robotic person. It is the tale of people who are no longer free and fully human. How easily we can be tempted by technology to give us a "quick fix," since we are desperate people living in turbulent times. But like all the wrong choices we are tempted to make, we suffer the consequences of poor decisions. In our surrender to technology, we have created for ourselves new forms of bondage while suffering the loss of human freedom.

> *In our surrender to technology, we have created for ourselves new forms of bondage while suffering the loss of human freedom.*

Technology has not brought Utopia. The Great Society of the sixties never emerged. Peace is still elusive, even in this post–Cold War era. We still do not know what form the "New World Order" will take. Poverty still exists. Racial strife and violence continue to tear our world apart. At the same time there are those, even within the church, who are without any firm conviction on what to base or rebuild their lives. Many who had a personal faith no longer do. Not only is faith gone, but there is nothing to take its place. Even though we can point to some acts of compassion, there is a loss of confidence among many. Although we are tempted to seek quick and easy solutions for our moral dilemma, yet we must resist the temptation and realize that no faith can survive unless it meets the double standard of intellectual validity and social relevance.

Temptation comes not only from the world around us, but it also comes to us from those who love and care for us. Of all the temptations, this is the hardest to resist. It comes from those who love us and have our best interest at heart, with not the slightest intention of harming us. You may be called by God to a special task or ministry, but are dissuaded by friends, who point out that it is a risky and unpopular pursuit. Such a decision in a worldly sense or within the business world would appear like wasting one's life and talent. Family members and close associates would point out that it appears that you are throwing your life away, wasting your talent when you could have a much more lucrative career. They define *success* in terms of financial security and affluence. That is a powerful temptation.

This is what happened to Jesus. His family tried to take him home. They thought he was mad. To them, he seemed to be throwing his life away. He was making a fool of himself, and they tried to stop him. They wanted him to quit what he was doing and come home with them. Amid this struggle Jesus said, "One's foes will be members of one's own household" (Matt. 10:36). Sometimes the most bitter temptation of all comes to us from the voices of those who love us.

Temptation may not come to us from our weakest point, but from our strongest point. We have a habit of saying, "That is one thing I will never do." What does that remind you of? It reminds us of Peter during the last week of Jesus' life. Peter said to Jesus in Gethsemane, prior to the crucifixion, "Though all become deserters because of you, I will never desert you" (Matt. 26:33), and then in almost the same breath, "Even though I must die with you, I will not deny you" (Matt. 26:35). Within hours, on three occasions he denied his Lord. Nothing gives temptation a foothold like overconfidence.

> *Nothing gives temptation a foothold*
> *like overconfidence.*

Temptation comes from within. It comes to us because it is able to appeal to something inside of us. Everyone has a weak spot. During a recent eye examination, I had my peripheral vision tested. When the ophthalmologist was going over the results of my examination, he pointed out that there was a place on the pattern where I had no vision. He said that is my blind spot, and that everyone has one. Just as we have a visual blind spot, so we also have a spiritual blind spot, and everyone has at least one. It is our point of vulnerability, which is different for each of us. What may have no effect on one person has an irresistible esffect on another. I believe that this is what Jesus is talking about in this part of the prayer, "Lead us not into temptation."

We have come to learn that the gospel involves suffering. Paul declared, "For he has graciously granted you the privilege not only of believing in Christ, but of suffering for him as well" (Phil. 1:29). Jesus constantly reminds us of the high cost of discipleship and that the "gate is narrow and the road is hard that leads to life, and there are few who find it" (Matt. 7:14). Jesus said there can be no hesitation, for "no one who puts a hand to the plow and looks back is fit for the kingdom of God" (Luke 9:62). Jesus speaks of discipleship as denying oneself and taking up the cross and following him. Jesus goes on to define discipleship in terms of servanthood by stating, "The greatest among you will be your servant" (Matt. 23:11). Unless we arm ourselves in advance for that moral, mental, or spiritual struggle, we will have little chance of survival when the test comes. Sin is conquered not in the moment of temptation but in the long, prayerful discipleship that precedes it.

In Gethsemane Jesus conquered the temptation to abandon the cross through all that went on before this moment—his baptism, the transfiguration, the long hours in prayer and the years of growing up in Nazareth. If the value structure and the moral foundation are not in place and the commitment made, then when the temptation comes we will fall.

In this portion of the Lord's Prayer, we are saying: "O Lord, I am not ready for this test or trial. I will fail. I will fall like Peter on the water; I will sink because I really don't have my eyes on you. Deliver me from that evil that seeks to do me harm. Help me to grow in grace and courage until I can face all things unafraid."

In this part of the Lord's Prayer, we learn the meaning of grace and love. Hendrik Kramer, the Dutch theologian, was contacted by several of his friends in 1939 in the Netherlands. They told him they were concerned because many of their Jewish friends were missing from their towns and villages. They asked Kramer what they ought to do. He said to them, "I cannot tell you what to do. But I can tell you who you are. If you know who you are you will know what to do." They went out and organized the Resistance movement. As trials and temptations come to us, we need to remember who we are, and then we will know how to act and what to do. We are sinners saved by grace. Therefore, "live your life in a manner worthy of the gospel of Christ" (Phil. 1:27).

At the beginning we talked about Archimedes. He said if he had a place to stand he could change the world. Amid the turbulence of temptation we need a place to stand. In difficult times we need a firm place to operate. Since the necessity of having such a starting point has long been recognized in both mathematics and science, how true it is in dealing with questions and experiences that affect our lives most deeply? Every set of logically connected propositions leads us back finally to some primitive proposition. The primary proposition for the Christian, the ultimate act of faith, is the trustworthiness of Jesus Christ. It is here that the Christian finds a place to stand.

CHAPTER EIGHT

Deliverance

*W*ithout a doubt Thomas Troeger was right on target when he said that we need "to see beneath the deceptive and often attractive appearance of evil. . . . We need courage to consider its ultimate source." There is both human decision and action behind every act of evil.

"Lay the cross on the ground near the hole. You pound the nails in the right hand, and I'll get the left. Then we'll do the feet." Something like this was said on the hillside at Calvary. Someone gave the orders. Someone had to see that the deed was done.

"You put the Zygon gas in the cylinders. I'll make sure the door is closed and the vents are sealed." Someone gave the orders at Auschwitz. Cold, detached words. Simple directions for the task at hand.

"Look out! Tanks have broken through the walls! Tear gas is seeping in! Get the gas masks! Here, you take the kerosene. Go that way! Take this can! Go the other way! Here's the torch." Someone at Waco gave the command—an inferno erupted.

I do not want to believe that men and women created in the image of God, created with such enormous capacity for good, could possess such a passion for evil.

Jesus prayed, "Deliver us from evil." We constantly struggle against evil. It pervades every aspect of our lives. We wrestle with it, trying to maintain our faith in a loving and caring God. Then desperate events, either experienced or reported, scream at us: "There is no such being!"

But we read in Genesis 1:26 that we all are made in the image of God—in goodness, love, and graciousness. Humans are made in the image of God with a marvelous capacity for good. On numerous occasions we have seen human life reflect the image of God in the darkest times, under the most difficult circumstances. From the bitter slavery of Pharaoh's brickyards; to the exile in Babylon; to the slopes of Calvary; to the ghettos of Poland; to the slums of Nicaragua; to the streets of Johannesburg, Soweto, Montgomery, and Little Rock—the universal goodness of the human spirit has prevailed even in the darkest times, under the most difficult circumstances. Even though death seems to nudge out life, darkness attempts to smother that light, and despair seeks to dispel all hope, still the reflection of the image of God in the human life prevails. In the face of evil's onslaught, "The light shines in the darkness, and the darkness did not overcome it" (John 1:5).

> *The universal goodness of the human spirit has prevailed even in the darkest times.*

Today, however, goodness is overshadowed by the human capacity for evil. Why? Because evil has the center stage in the media. Crime and brutality get prime time and top billing. The dark side of life grabs the headlines in today's dailies, because this is what sells newspapers. And the fact remains that there is a great deal of evil going on in our world at an ever-alarming rate. One critic has keenly pointed out that a generation of preaching about peace of mind, self-esteem, successful living, and confidence that "all is well" is now colliding with the silent cynicism of a popular culture that dismisses religious belief as whistling in the dark. This cynicism is modified by a stoicism that simply accepts evil as inevitable.

I am aware that evil consciously and unconsciously affects our lives. Every congregation includes persons who are over-whelmed by evil, either through mental illness, depression, physical pain, loss of the meaning and direction of life, or the evil deeds of others. Then there are persons who are making a silent protest; even though singing the hymns and repeating the prayers and liturgy, they have difficulty recognizing a loving God with what is going on in the world around them.

Recently, we witnessed the dedication of the Holocaust Memorial in Washington, D.C. As I listened to the speeches and remarks of the participants, many who were the survivors of the Holocaust, I realized how close to the surface of our world are the same feelings and attitudes that produced the Holocaust nearly fifty years ago. This is why today the atroci-ties in Bosnia and Rwanda send cold chills down our spines.

Then there is our own struggle with good and evil. It is akin to that of the apostle Paul in Romans 7:19: "For I do not do the good I want, but the evil I do not want is what I do." We know exactly what the apostle is talking about. We have the ability to see what is good, but the inability to do it. Paul describes himself as frustrated, having a split personality, a walking civil war. Evil was a personal problem for the apostle Paul. It is a serious problem for us.

"Deliver us from evil." We recite these words every time we repeat the Lord's Prayer. Most of the time when we pray these words, we mean to pray, "Deliver us from the bad things that may happen to us." We are asking that we not be the victims of evil.

> *Most of the time when we pray these words, we mean to pray, "Deliver us from the bad things that may happen to us."*

But evil is an equation that can be viewed from two sides: the evil we suffer, and the evil we do. The question is From which side of that equation do we most need deliverance?

Although we usually pray for deliverance from the evil that could possibly happen to us, how much more do we need to pray for deliverance from the evil we do. But we are church people. We recite creeds, read scriptures, and repeat prayers that deal with goodness, truth, and justice. From what evil could we possibly need deliverance?

Not all evil deeds are performed by evil people. The political and social struggle in the second half of this century in South America introduced a new phrase in contemporary theology: "social sin." To the Latin American bishops who were in the forefront of this struggle, it was clear that the worst kinds of evil were not to be found in the acts of individuals, but in social structures. Catholic theologian Robert Ellsberg points out that "there is little difference between violence that kills a child with a gun, and violence that causes death by starvation" ("Truth Makes Demands of Us," *The Living Pulpit* [Oct.-Dec. 1992]: 16f.). The greatest evil may not be performed with any consciousness of evil intent. Some social structures have systematic effects that guarantee massive suffering and misery. These structures on numerous occasions have had our blessings and support.

Ellsberg concludes that for us to be delivered from evil may not mean that we are rescued from its effect. It may not even mean that evil is eradicated. It may mean that we are able to see it, recognize it, name it for what it is, even when—especially when—we are not its principal victims.

> *The worst kinds of evil are not to be found in the acts of individuals, but in social structures.*

Tom Troeger tells the story of a preacher friend of his who pastored a church in a small town. When the preacher first entered the town where his parish was located, he was impressed by the sign at the city limits: "Welcome to our city of peace and friendship." But as he settled in he discovered that seething under all that "peace and friendship" was a deep-seated racial bigotry and hatred. He said it was reinforced by a small group of men who met regularly in an exclusive social club. Evil existed under the cloak of apparent decency. Pascal declared, "Men never do evil so completely and cheerfully as when they do it from religious conviction."

"Deliver us from evil." This is not simply the cry of people who are the victims of evil but the prayer of people who bring pain and misery into the lives of others, not with weapons of violence but with our silence or indifference, our lack of curiosity. It was Edmund Burke who said, "The only thing necessary for the triumph of evil is for good men to do nothing."

"Evil grows invisible because we are part of it." Those were the words of Albert Speer, the architect who helped to build the Third Reich. He was the only defendant at the Nuremburg trials to accept full responsibility for the charges brought against him, even for acts of which he was ignorant. He wrote later, "If I was ignorant, I ensured my own ignorance. If I did not see, it was because I did not want to see." He said, "The evil was invisible because I was part of it."

Lord, deliver us from that evil that is so hard for us to see, because we are part of it. How is this possible? How can that happen to us? Because we see people who are different from us—as those "other people." The stranger next door. The neighbor with whom we never speak. Someone who is intrinsically different—the "other." Someone we consider less than ourselves—expendable.

How easily the homeless can become invisible to us. We lose sight of the pervasive reality of poverty and homelessness, because we do not see or recognize these people as human beings like us, but merely the "other." They are invisible. "Deliver us from evil," the evil that is impossible for us to see because we are so much a part of it. That is the cruelest evil of all.

David was the king of Israel. He was popular and powerful. He had been resting on his couch following a military victory when he saw what he wanted, a very beautiful woman. Her name was Bathsheba, and she was the wife of Uriah, one of David's generals. It was at this point that David should have prayed, "Lord, deliver me from this evil, before I become ensnared." But as Walter Brueggemann points out, David acted swiftly, as he always did. He was not a pensive or brooding man, but one who would have his way, and his action was quick. The verbs in the narrative rush as David's passion rushes: He saw. He sent. He took. He lay. It is an all-too-familiar story of a man who had an affair with another man's wife. When she became pregnant, David's action to hide the affair was so stark. There is no hint of caring, no affection or love—only lust.

David got what he wanted. There was no restraint, no second thoughts, no reservation. What was he to do about her husband, Uriah? One evil deed quickly led to another. As the commander-in-chief, David called in Joab, one of his commanders, and instructed him to place Uriah in the front line where the fighting was the heaviest. Then Joab was to pull his troops back, leaving Uriah unprotected, at the mercy of the enemy. Joab did as he was instructed, like a good soldier, and drew his troops back, leaving Uriah alone to face the enemy. Joab reported to David that Uriah had been killed. The deed was done. Uriah is dead, and Bathsheba was now David's. No remorse. No pain or anguish of conscience. His evil grew invisible, because he was so much a part of it. There was no thought of evil on David's part.

The Lord sent Nathan to David. He told David a story about two men who lived in a certain village. One was rich and the other was poor. The rich man had many flocks and herds. The poor man had nothing, except one lamb that he had bought with all the money he had. The lamb grew up with his children. The lamb ate from his table and drank from his cup; it was like one of the children to the man.

Now, a traveler came to the rich man's house, and he wanted to prepare a meal for his visitor. Instead of taking a lamb from his own flock, he took the poor man's only lamb, killed it, and prepared a feast for his friend. When David heard the story, he was angry at the rich man. He told Nathan that the rich man deserved to die for what he had done. He said that no pity should be shown toward that man. Nathan said to David, "You are the man!"

For the first time David realized that he had committed a monstrous evil against Bathsheba, violating her woman-hood, and against her husband, committing adultery. David said to Nathan, "I have sinned against the Lord."

The point of Jesus' prayer "Deliver us from evil" reveals to us that Jesus is concerned not about explaining evil, but about overcoming it. The Lord who teaches us to pray these immensely powerful words, "Deliver us from evil," is the One who can do it.

CHAPTER NINE

*All your works shall give thanks to you, O LORD,
and all your faithful shall bless you.
They shall speak of the glory of your kingdom,
and tell of your power,
to make known to all people your mighty deeds,
and the glorious splendor of your kingdom.
Your kingdom is an everlasting kingdom,
and your dominion endures throughout all
generations.
(Ps. 145:10-13)*

The Kingdom, the Power, and the Glory

For thine is the kingdom, and the power, and the glory for ever." This is the final phrase of the Lord's Prayer. It is not part of the original prayer taught by Jesus. It is not found in any of the New Testament manuscripts, but is usually consigned to a foot-note. It was not in general use until the seventeenth century, when it first appeared in the Scottish *Book of Common Prayer* in 1637. Since that time it has been widely used in Protestant churches. The Roman Catholic version ends as it does in Matthew 6 with the phrase "deliver us from evil." A possibly earlier usage was the practice of the early church to respond to the hearing of the Lord's Prayer by saying, "For thine is the kingdom, and the power, and the glory for ever. Amen." Does it really matter that these are not the words of Jesus himself? John Killinger tells the story about the final months of Mozart's life, when he was commissioned to write a requiem mass for a citizen of Vienna. He worked intensely to complete the opening section, but his chronic cough grew worse and he fell into a weakened condition, at the point of exhaustion. He died before he completed the mass and was buried in a pauper's grave. It was difficult for his students to allow the requiem to remain unfinished and unsung. So they slavishly spent long hours studying his notes and technique until finally they completed the requiem. When it is performed today with all of its lyric beauty it is considered the work of Mozart, and the praise is given to the famous composer and not to his students. Killinger concludes the story by saying, "So it is with the final phrase of the Lord's Prayer. Even though they are not the words of Jesus, they are the testimony of his followers to the truth of his vision and the reality of the kingdom that he preached" (*The God Named Hallowed* [Nashville: Abingdon Press, 1988], 74).

> *Christians were adding to the words of Jesus a sign of their own agreement with and enthusiasm for the kingdom.*

It is conceivable that these closing words were quoted from either 1 Chronicles 29; Psalm 145; or Romans 11. Whatever the source, Christians were adding to the words of Jesus a sign of their own agreement with and enthusiasm for the kingdom. They were adding the words of their testimony, because the kingdom was the center of everything for them.

The kingdom that they prayed for was foremost in their lives, was the kingdom that had come, and that is coming. E. Stanley Jones, the great Methodist missionary to India, visited Russia just after the Second World War. He said of all he heard and saw that it was like a great prison of the human spirit. Life was dreary and depressing. During his prayer time, a Bible verse leaped out at him: "Therefore, since we are receiving a kingdom that cannot be shaken, let us give thanks" (Heb. 12:28). He pointed out that this is not only a kingdom that "will not be shaken" but a kingdom that "cannot be shaken." He saw in a flash that all kingdoms are shakable. They are held together by purges and force, and if these are relaxed, the kingdom will crumble. He felt then that Communism's days were numbered. How prophetic he was, although he never lived to see the demise of Communism in the Soviet Union. The kingdom of capitalism is shakable. It is at the mercy of the daily fluctuations of the stock market, which ever reacts to world events; it is so vulnerable and so fragile. Jones points out that the kingdom of self is just as shakable. If you center on yourself, the self will sour and go to pieces. When you are all wrapped up in yourself, you make a small package indeed. Jones concludes that everything is shakable except one thing: the kingdom of God.

The words of "kingdom, power, and glory" are words we need to hear during times of despair and disappointment. There is a feeling among us that everything is coming apart. Why is there such a boom in doom? Books on the end of time, the rapture, the Second Coming, numerology, and apocalypticism are in great demand, especially as this century draws to a close. The reason for their popularity stems from the current mood that we have lost control over our lives and that the world is in a state of disarray. We have the feeling that the present way of life may end and the destruction of life as we know it is at hand. The current mood among so many is that we can no longer determine our destiny and we feel paralyzed in the face of these destructive forebodings. Sermons, books, and writings that offer simple and direct answers have great appeal. These popular views of apocalypticism (I would define *apocalypticism* as the forecasting of the ultimate destiny and doom of the world) are expressed within the framework of both a rational account of terror along with a prescription for survival. The lure of such apocalypticism provides one with a confident mastery over an ominous future. There is no doubt that even the most optimistic persons among us have deep concerns for things as they are. The things within our world, community, and our personal lives weigh heavily upon us.

For the pessimist the world's only continuity is its endless variation. A professor from one of our universities told me that the lack of answers in regard to justice and morality has caused him to abandon the church and his faith in God. He was convinced that religion was the cause of the problems in Northern Ireland, the Middle East, and the longstanding conflict between the Jews and the Palestinians. Who could argue with that? He was convinced that questions about morality are not religious questions but are philosophical and should be addressed by the experts on the subject—the professors of philosophy. Convinced that religion was irrelevant, he had abandoned his personal faith in God.

This professor's despair is our despair. God never expects us to close our minds and pretend that the world of conflict and ambiguity does not exist. What does life mean in a world like ours where we see only through "a glass darkly" and at best with only partial knowledge? It is here in this world of the fleeting, transient, and fragile, that we hope to discover the permanent, the durable, and the eternal. We do live in two worlds, one that will pass away and one that will abide forever. May God help us to distinguish between the two. It is here that we discover God, who is the "same yesterday, today and forever." It is at this point that the closing words of the Lord's Prayer, "kingdom, power, glory," take on new meaning. The highest use that we can make of a shaken time is to discover the unshakable.

This closing doxology is one of hope. During a period of history when it was dangerous to be a Christian, even life threatening, it is understandable what meaning this phrase had. The hope of the early Christians was in the steadfast love of God, which raises the dead and transforms human life and society, filling the earth with God's righteousness, freedom, and peace. Their hope was not only to see God but to serve, glorify, and enjoy God forever. Christian hope, faith, and love appropriately end in doxology: "For thine is the kingdom, the power and the glory for ever!"

There is an inclusiveness to this part of the Lord's Prayer in that it relates to all of life, in that it can be prayed under any conditions, even amid the stress and strain of the family—especially within the single-parent family. It is meaningful in those critical moments when the familiar is disappearing from our lives; when the company is moving you to a strange place and you say good-bye to friends and loved ones; when you stand in line for an unemployment check; when the doctor tells you that your illness is terminal; even when you must lower the body of a loved one into a grave. It is then that you can repeat the doxology, "For thine is the kingdom, the power, and the glory," with both meaning and conviction.

For many of us, these are the words with which we have grown up. This phrase became familiar to us early in life. It has been etched deeply upon us, taught to us by loved ones who are now gone. We have heard these words at baptisms, Holy Communion, weddings, and funerals. In the most precious moments we have shared as families, these words have been with us. They have galvanized the courage of our parents. The meaning of these words has stood by us in our world of change as things come and go, but the truth of these words remains with us.

> *The meaning of these words has stood by us in our world of change as things come and go, but the truth of these words remains with us.*

Such words stood by my friend Dale Doss, a member of a church I once pastored. One Sunday Dale gave his witness before the congregation. He was a Naval officer, serving as an attack bombardier in the Vietnam war. He was shot down over North Vietnam and captured by peasant farmers, who turned him over to the North Vietnam army. He was placed in a prison camp, infamous as the Hanoi Hilton, but known to the Vietnamese as Hao-Loi, meaning "fiery furnace." He remained there for five years. He told the congregation how on numerous occasions he was suspended by ropes tied to his arms and legs, pulling his shoulder and hip sockets out of joint. He was held in a cell that was freezing cold in the winter and unbearably hot and humid in the summer. He told us how he was isolated for two years in solitary confinement. When he was taken from his cell for interrogation, he was usually beaten. He told us that he never broke down to the enemy, not because of his strength but because of God's strength, which came to him by what had happened years earlier in his life as a child.

He grew up in a poor family in Alabama. While his mother worked, his grandmother took care of him. Many times she made him sit in a straight-back chair while she washed clothes in a washtub. There she taught him hymns and Scripture, especially Psalm 23 and the Lord's Prayer. He remembered her telling him, "Dale, someday they will have meaning for you." Little did he know then what that meaning would be. It was there that he learned the words of the Lord's Prayer by heart.

Dale said that he remained sane during those years as a prisoner of war by repeating the words of Scripture and the Lord's Prayer and singing the hymns that his grandmother had taught him. Little did his grandmother know what significance those moments would have for her grandson in such a faraway place and under such circumstances. In simple piety, through prayer and teaching, she gave her grandson something to live by during the most trying time of his life. Without it, Dale admitted, he would never have survived.

Parents will never fully know the influence of their nurturing. Our children and grandchildren look up at us as we stand in worship and recite creeds with big, strange-sounding words, and listen to us as we sing the hymns and repeat the prayers. Although they do not understand, they remember that at that moment it all appeared so important to us. There may come a time when they will understand why.

The Lord's Prayer ends with a final word—*Amen!* This word is found throughout the Bible. In the Hebrew it means "so be it." In the Old Testament liturgy, it was a response of the people, a corporate expression of unity—"We agree." It has the same meaning in the New Testament, expressing agreement on what has been said or done. Early Methodists were known for their chorus of "amens," which were characteristic of their worship. It was their way of expressing agreement.

After repeating the Lord's Prayer and saying the final phrase, "Thine is the kingdom, and the power and the glory," we tie it all together in one final word of agreement: *Amen!*

You can walk away from disappointment, brokenness, and heartache; from a broken relationship; from a hospital room; from a graveside, because after praying "Thine is the kingdom, the power and the glory" you can then say "Amen."

So be it!

Bibliography

Ayo, Nicholas. *The Lord's Prayer*. South Bend, Ind.: University of Notre Dame Press, 1992.

Barclay, William. *The Beatitudes and the Lord's Prayer for Everyman*. New York, Harper & Row: 1968.

———. *The Plain Man Looks at the Lord's Prayer*. Glasgow: Collins, 1964.

Boff, Leonardo. *The Lord's Prayer*. Maryknoll, N.Y.: Orbis, 1983.

Chase, Frederick. *The Lord's Prayer in the Early Church*. London: Cambridge University Press, 1967.

Davidson, John A. *The Lord's Prayer*. New York: World Publishing, 1970.

Ebeling, Gerhard. *The Lord's Prayer in Today's World*. London: SCM Press, 1966.

Fosdick, Harry Emerson. *The Meaning of Prayer*. New York: Doubleday, 1951.

Foster, Richard J. *Prayer*. San Francisco: Harper, 1992.

Harner, Philip. *Understanding the Lord's Prayer*. Philadelphia: Fortress, 1975.

Harper, Steve. *Praying Through the Lord's Prayer*. Nashville: The Upper Room, 1992.

BIBLIOGRAPHY

Jeremias, Joachim. *The Lord's Prayer.* Philadelphia: Fortress, 1964.

———. *Abba: The Prayers of Jesus.* Philadelphia: Fortress, 1978.

Killinger, John. *The God Named Hallowed: The Lord's Prayer for Today.* Nashville: Abingdon Press, 1988.

Laymon, Charles M. *The Lord's Prayer in Biblical Setting.* Nashville: Abingdon Press, 1968.

The Living Pulpit 2, 3 (July-September 1993). The entire issue on prayer, with articles on the Lord's Prayer.

Schriver, Donald W. *The Lord's Prayer: A Way of Life.* Atlanta: John Knox Press, 1983.

Scott, Ernest F. *The Lord's Prayer: Its Character, Purpose and Interpretation.* New York: Charles Scribner's Sons, 1951.

Thielicke, Helmut. *Our Heavenly Father: Sermons on the Lord's Prayer.* Translated by John Doberstein. New York: Harper and Bros., 1960.

Trueblood, Elton. *The Lord's Prayers.* New York: Harper and Bros., 1965.

Underhill, Evelyn. *Abba: Meditations Based on the Lord's Prayer.* London: Longman and Green, 1940.